STAR WARS
THE
MANDALORIAN

After decades of terror and oppression, the Galactic Empire is no more, and the New Republic has risen in its wake. Lurking in the outskirts of space, beyond governmental authority, a legendary bounty hunter known as the Mandalorian lives by an ancient code, in a ruthless fight for survival. But when commissioned to retrieve a precious asset for a mysterious client, the gunfighter soon realizes that evil is still out there, tough and resilient like beskar steel.

This is the way... to learning everything about the Mandalorian! Through on-set anecdotes, fun facts, production photos and original concept art, this collector's edition will take you on a journey across the Outer Rim Territories. Find out everything about the Child, new planets and means of transport, and become a full member of Mando's clan.

TITAN EDITORIAL
Editor Jonathan Wilkins
Managing Editor Martin Eden
Art Director Oz Browne
Senior Designer Andrew Leung
Assistant Editor Phoebe Hedges
Production Controller Caterina Falqui
Production Controller Kelly Fenlon
Production Manager Jackie Flook
Sales and Circulation Manager Steve Tothill
Sales and Marketing Coordinator George Wickenden
Marketing and Advertisement Assistant Lauren Noding
Publicist Imogen Harris
Aquisitions Editor Duncan Baizley
Publishing Director Ricky Claydon
Publishing Director John Dziewiatkowski
Operations Director Leigh Baulch
Publishers Nick Landau and Vivian Cheung

DISTRIBUTION
U.S. Newsstand: Total Publisher Services, Inc.
John Dziewiatkowski, 630-851-7683
U.S. Distribution: Ingrams Periodicals,
Curtis Circulation Company
U.K. Newsstand: Marketforce, 0203 787 9199
U.S./U.K. Direct Sales Market: Diamond Comic Distributors
For more info on advertising contact adinfo@titanemail.com

Contents © 2021 Lucasfilm Ltd. & TM. All Rights Reserved

First edition: May 2021

Star Wars: The Mandalorian: Guide to Season One: The Official Collector's Edition is published by Titan Magazines, a division of Titan Publishing Group Limited, 144 Southwark Street, London, SE1 0UP
Printed in the U.S.A.

For sale in the U.S., Canada, U.K., and Eire

ISBN: 9781787737105
Titan Authorized User.
TMN 14092

No part of this publication may be reproduced, stored in a retrival system, or transmitted, in any form or by any means, without the prior written permission of the publisher.

A CIP catalogue record for this title is available from the British Library.

10 9 8 7 6 5 4 3 2 1

LUCASFILM EDITORIAL
Senior Editor Robert Simpson
Art Director Troy Alders
Creative Director Michael Siglain
Story Group Leland Chee, Pablo Hidalgo
Creative Art Manager Phil Szostak
Asset Management Bryce Pinkos, Chris Argyropoulos, Erik Sanchez, Gabrielle Levenson, Jason Schultz, Nicole LaCoursiere, Sarah Williams
Special Thanks: Lynne Hale, Christopher Troise, Eugene Paraszczuk

CONTENTS

THE GALAXY

1 /

IMPERIAL DOMINION

Rising from the ashes of the Old Republic, the First Galactic Empire was officially established at the end of the Clone Wars. Supreme Chancellor Sheev Palpatine proclaimed himself Galactic Emperor and started to rule the galaxy through fear and tyranny. To further centralize the power in his hands, the Emperor dismantled the Senate and transferred its responsibilities to Moffs and regional governors, who would report directly to him.

THE FALL

Scattered across the galaxy, small resistance groups began to spring up. They ultimately came together as a single movement intended to destroy the Empire. The Alliance to Restore the Republic was officially born. After years of strenuous and bitter conflict, the rebels managed to successfully defeat the Galactic Empire in the battles of Endor and Jakku, thus bringing the galaxy to freedom. At long last, the Galactic Civil War was over.

2 /

IMPERIAL REMNANTS

Democracy was restored. The Rebel Alliance reinstated the Galactic Senate as the primary ruling body of the New Republic. While the newly-formed Republic strived to regain control and reconvene the Senate in the inner regions of the galaxy, surviving Imperial warlords and devotees were scattered across the Outer Rim planets, out of the government's reach.

A RISING UNDERWORLD

Imperial survivors and their plans to restore the Galactic Empire by force aren't the Republic's only concern. In the remote, lawless outskirts of the galaxy, mercenaries, bounty hunters and criminal syndicates began to operate freely, making their own rules in a ruthless fight for survival. Anything and anyone could be sold for the right price. Amongst them, a mysterious bounty hunter with an obscure past and a big reputation: the Mandalorian. ✠

3 /

1 / Supreme Chancellor Palpatine announces the birth of the Galactic Empire.

2 / Heroes of the Rebellion celebrate the Empire's defeat.

3 / The Imperial emblem on the Client's medallion leaves no doubt about his affiliation.

4 / The bounty hunter known as the Mandalorian locates a target on an icy planet.

4 /

EPISODE SUMMARY

CHAPTER 1: THE MANDALORIAN

A few years after the fall of the Empire, a Mandalorian bounty hunter delivers targets to Guild agent Greef Karga on the planet Nevarro. He then accepts an assignment from a mysterious client, who wants him to hunt down an unnamed asset. The Mandalorian leaves for Arvala-7, where an Ugnaught named Kuiil points him to the bounty's location. The Mandalorian travels to a guarded encampment and teams up with IG-11, a droid after the same target, to clear the area. Once inside, they realize the bounty is actually an infant. The droid attempts to kill the asset, but the Mandalorian shoots him, thus saving the youngling.

CHAPTER 2: THE CHILD

Going back with the bounty, the Mandalorian finds some Jawas looting the *Razor Crest*, his ship. After a fight, they manage to escape on their sandcrawler. At Kuiil's suggestion, the gunfighter negotiates with the scavengers to trade the stolen parts for a mudhorn's egg. After finding its cave, the Mandalorian is severely attacked by the beast. The mudhorn prepares for the death blow but is suddenly stopped by the infant, who uses a mysterious power to immobilize it. This gives enough time to the Mandalorian to stop the beast. The hunter repairs his ship and finally leaves the planet along with the Child.

3 /

1 /

1 / The renowned bounty hunter known as the Mandalorian arrives on an ice planet. Concept art by Nick Gindraux.

2 / Frenemies and hunters IG-11 and Mando on Arvala-7. Concept art by Christian Alzmann.

2 /

CHAPTER 3: THE SIN

The Mandalorian delivers the Child to the Client. He then returns to a secret Mandalorian enclave, where the Armorer forges a new cuirass and weapons with the reward beskar—the steel which Mandalorian armors are made of. After taking a new commission, the bounty hunter asks Karga what will happen to the infant, but the agent reminds him that asking questions is forbidden. The gunfighter prepares for his next job, but just before leaving he changes his mind and heads back to the Client's safehouse, where he rescues the Child. While returning to the ship, he is assaulted by other bounty hunters and Karga. The Mandalorian is critically outnumbered, until fellow Mandalorians show up and fight the opponents, giving him time to reach the ship and escape safely with the Child.

3 / The Mandalorian takes the bounty back to his ship on Arvala-7. Concept art by John Park.

4 / The Mandalorian enters the Client's safehouse on Nevarro. Concept art by Nick Gindraux.

CHAPTER 4: SANCTUARY

In search of a place to lie low, the Mandalorian and the Child travel to Sorgan, where they meet mercenary Cara Dune. Later, the hunter is approached by some farmers who need help to run some raiders off their village. Both the Mandalorian and Cara Dune agree to help and teach them to shoot and fight. Then, they set up a trap for the raiders' AT-ST, managing to blow it up. Unable to use their main weapon, the raiders flee. With peace restored to the village, the Mandalorian considers leaving the Child with the farmers, but Dune spots and kills a bounty hunter aiming at him who is also after the Child. Understanding that the Guild has tracked them down, the Mandalorian and the Child leaves Sorgan.

5 / Sorgan farmers lure the raiders' AT-ST into a trap. Concept art by Christian Alzmann.

6 / Young Toro Calican and Mando comb Tatooine's deserts in search of assassin Fennec Shand. Concept art by Ryan Church.

7 / Aboard the prison transport, Ranzar Malk's crew and Mando confront the New Republic security droids. Concept art by Nick Gindraux.

6 /

CHAPTER 5: THE GUNSLINGER

In need of repairs to his ship, the Mandalorian lands on a repair bay on Tatooine, run by mechanic Peli Motto. The gunfighter asks her to watch the Child while he searches for a job to pay for repairs. He then joins novice bounty hunter Toro Calican in tracking down dangerous assassin Fennec Shand. The hunters capture Shand in the desert, but one of their speeder bikes gets destroyed in the fight. Once the Mandalorian leaves to find a new transport, Shand asks Calican to set her free: in return, she'll help him catch the Mandalorian, who has a much higher bounty on his head. Calican blasts her and leaves for the repair dock. There, he takes the Child and Motto as hostages, but the Mandalorian, who arrives shortly after, blasts him. After paying Motto, the Mandalorian leaves Tatooine with the Child.

CHAPTER 6: THE PRISONER

Looking for work, the Mandalorian visits his former partner Ranzar Malk in his space station. Together with Mayfeld, an ex-Imperial sharpshooter, droid Q9-0, blade-expert Xi'an, and Devaronian Burg, the gunfighter goes on a mission to rescue Qin, Xian's brother, who's been caught by the New Republic. The team infiltrates the prison ship, but as soon as they find Qin the other mercenaries betray the Mandalorian and trap him inside the craft. However, the gunfighter outsmarts the crew and escapes, taking Qin to Malk and leaving the others behind. Once the Mandalorian has left with the reward, Malk readies a gunship to kill him, but the Mandalorian proves, once again, to be smarter and manages to get away safely.

7 /

CHAPTER 7:
THE RECKONING

Greef Karga sends a transmission to the Mandalorian and informs him that the Client has besieged Nevarro. He then asks for his help to terminate him: in return, the bounty hunter will be cleared with the Guild. The Mandalorian flies to Nevarro together with Dune and Kuiil, who brings along a reprogrammed IG-11 to guard the Child. The group heads to the settlement, but reptavians suddenly attack Karga. Severely injured, the agent is saved by the Child, who uses the Force to heal him. The team sets up a plan: Karga will bring the Mandalorian and the Child's empty cradle to the client, while Kuiil will get the kid to safety. During the meeting, former Imperial Moff Gideon appears and attacks the gathering, killing the Client. In the meantime, two of Gideon's scout troopers find Kuiil and kidnap the Child.

8 / The Imperial Remnant's leader Moff Gideon escorted by his death trooper guards lands on Nevarro. Concept art by Brian Matyas and Doug Chiang.

CHAPTER 8: REDEMPTION

IG-11 saves the Child from the troopers and heads to the Nevarro common house to rescue his friends. During the fight, Gideon manages to injure the Mandalorian. While the others escape, IG-11 stays with the bounty hunter and heals him. Rejoining the others, the Mandalorian learns that Gideon's troops attacked his covert. The Mandalorian Armorer, amongst the few survivors, tells him that the Child must be reunited with its kind and cared for until then. The group escapes through a lava river, and IG-11 self-destructs to kill all the enemies. Aboard his TIE fighter, Gideon attacks the group, but the bounty hunter manages to take him down. Now safe, the Mandalorian and the Child part ways with Dune and Karga and leave. Meanwhile, the Moff, who has survived, cuts himself out of the TIE with the Darksaber. ⚓

9 / The Mandalorian
takes Moff Gideon's
TIE fighter down.
Concept art by
Christian Alzmann.

THE MANDALORIAN

With a mysterious past hidden beneath a gleaming beskar helmet, the Mandalorian is a person of action, not one of words. A lone and skillful warrior with a strong reputation and an even stronger drive and determination, he's one of the greatest bounty hunters of the Outer Rim Territories. Utterly ruthless with his enemies, the Mandalorian still retains a heart capable of compassion—especially when it comes to a tiny, moon-eyed being with big, protruding ears…

THE LORE OF MANDALORE

The impenetrable warriors known as Mandalorians share a history of glory, struggle, and decline. Originally living on Mandalore, a planet located in the Outer Rim Territories, Mandalorians were famous across the galaxy for their military skills. Their social organization in clans and houses led to several civil conflicts which utterly wrecked the planet, turning it into a desert wasteland. After many battles, Mandalore fell under the control of both the Galactic Republic and the Empire.

1 /

2 /

1 / The horned mythosaur skull became one of the symbols of Mandalorians.

2 / The Mandalorian has never removed his helmet in front of other living beings.

3 / The helmets of the fallen Mandalorians on Nevarro.

3 /

4 /

4 / During an attack on their hometown, Djarin's parents hid their son under a hatch to save his life.

5 / The Mandalorian checks a tracking fob inside the cockpit of the *Razor Crest*.

6 / Young Djarin was rescued by a Mandalorian warrior.

During the Imperial era, in a conflict known as The Great Purge, the Empire exterminated most of the Mandalorian people, taking possession of beskar—a highly valuable alloy, which can withstand extreme damage. After the fall of the Empire, Mandalorians were believed to be extinct, yet a small number of warriors managed to survive. Amongst them, a congregation of Mandalorians living in a covert and operating in great secrecy on Nevarro. After the Imperial survivors hiding on the planet learned of their existence, most of them were exterminated and the survivors were forced to flee the enclave. Their actual location is unknown.

FROM DJARIN TO MANDO

Underneath his shiny armor, the Mandalorian, born as Din Djarin, bears the burden of a difficult past. During the Clone Wars, Separatist battle droids attacked Djarin's hometown when he was just a child. His parents managed to hide him from the attackers, dying in an explosion shortly after. The kid was then rescued by a Mandalorian warrior, who used his jetpack to carry Djarin away from the battlefield, thus saving his life. In accordance with their creed, Mandalorians raised the 'foundling' as a member of the clan, teaching him their way of life and training him in the Fighting Corps. Once of age, Djarin adhered to their strict code of conduct defined as The Way. These Mandalorians are forbidden to remove their helmets in front of other living beings, nor can they have it removed by someone else; otherwise, they wouldn't be able to put it on again. After joining the Bounty Hunters Guild, the Mandalorian quickly became one of its most valuable warriors, collecting bounties across the outer systems aboard his trusted gunship, the *Razor Crest*.

BESKAR HEART

A seasoned warrior hardened by years of battles and solitude, the Mandalorian doesn't have time—nor words—to waste. Despite being acknowledged as the best bounty hunter in the business, the Mandalorian never enjoys his success, preferring to focus on his following commission instead. Secretive and withdrawn, he is often distrustful of others and suspicious of their motives. Especially droids. He has a strong aversion to them, presumably due to the encounter in his early childhood, with a super battle droid who attempted to kill him. He's not very fond of Jawas, either—particularly when they dismantle his ship to sell its parts or when they mock his Jawa language skills. Yet, he's capable of expressing gratitude to those few who manage to earn his trust and respect. Highly devoted to Mandalorians for having raised him as one of their own, Mando shows consideration for orphan children under their care. Indeed, he apportions some of his earnings from bounty hunting to the Armorer, who sets it aside for the future of the foundlings.

7 / As a former foundling himself, Mando quickly bonded with the Child.

8 / Mando walking through Nevarro's market. As a bounty hunter, he must be alert at all times.

7 /

8 /

ARMOR AND WEAPONS

9 / Mando's Amban sniper rifle proved very useful when fighting a huge ravinak on an icy planet.

10 / The Mandalorian showing his weaponry to the stormtroopers guarding the Client.

11 / In combat, Mando can count on several tricks up his sleeve.

To Mandalorians, armor is more than a metal covering to wear in battle: it is, in fact, a part of their identity and culture, something that makes them immediately recognizable by fellow warriors and enemies alike. In this regard, Mando's gear is no exception.

Following the Mandalorian tradition, he wears a helmet with a T-shaped visor equipped with a macrobinocular viewplate, shoulder pauldrons, gauntlets, vambraces, a cuirass, a cape, and a bandolier. After receiving a camtono of beskar steel from the Client when he recovered and delivered the Child, Mando managed to replace his damaged armor with a full set.

Weapons are equally important, for they are, as stated by Mando himself, part of the Mandalorian religion. Indeed, the bounty hunter has plenty of weaponry at his disposal, such as a blaster pistol, a vibro-knife and an Amban sniper rifle – which can also be used as a taser or a sonic detector if needed. Further to this, Mando has also got several tricks up his sleeve: a whipcord launcher, dual flamethrowers and whistling birds—tiny missiles useful for striking multiple targets simultaneously. Before leaving Nevarro to reunite the Child with his people, the Mandalorian also receives a long-coveted device: a jetpack, often used by Mandalorian warriors as well as by other armed forces.

BEHIND THE SCENES

The concept art of Boba Fett—the first character to wear Mandalorian armor in a *Star Wars* film—was influenced from the "Man With No Name"—the character played by Clint Eastwood in three western movies by Sergio Leone. The same iconography inspired the design of Mando, making him a character full of mystery. Therefore, it is no coincidence that actor Pedro Pascal watched several samurai and western movies by Akira Kurosawa and Sergio Leone to get into the character, and was heavily inspired by Clint Eastwood in films such as *The Good, The Bad and the Ugly* (1966). Pascal truly reached for the stars when it came to enhancing his performance: right before rehearsing for the season finale, the actor injured himself while walking out of the makeup trailer.

As he was about to film the 'unmasking' scene with droid IG-11, Pascal went to the hospital with his face covered in fake blood and wounds, unsurprisingly alarming the hospital personnel. Seven stitches later, however, the actor went back on set and shot the scene as originally planned, thus proving to be as tough and heroic as only a true Mandalorian would be. But Pedro Pascal was not the only one who portrayed the Mandalorian in the series. He actually modeled his performance around the physicality of his stunt doubles: Brendan Wayne, the weapons expert, who took care of the gunslinger aspect; and Lateef Crowder, the martial arts expert, who performed the fighting sequences. Therefore, the Mandalorian is the result of the work of three different people who act as one. ⚓

12 / Pre-production shot showing different Mandalorian helmets in the making.

13 / Actor Pedro Pascal and actress Misty Rosas learning the art of blurrg riding.

14 / Shooting the 'mudhorn fight' scene.

15 / The Mandalorian's combat sequences were performed by martial arts expert Lateef Crowder.

16 / Pedro Pascal lending his beskar helmet to series creator and executive producer Jon Favreau.

17 / The Mandalorian aims Gideon's E-Web heavy repeating blaster cannon against the Moff's own stormtroopers.

THE CHILD

This green-skinned, tiny being known as "the Child" is the most sought-after bounty in the galaxy; luckily, he can count on quite the unexpected ally—the Mandalorian—and on an incredible power—which he has yet to fully master—to keep from becoming an Imperial prisoner and test subject. Despite being 50 years old he is still a child, unable to speak any known language and in need of someone to take care of him...

A BABY WRAPPED IN SECRECY

From his origins to his name, everything about the Child is shrouded in mystery. His physical features—green skin, wrinkly face and wide, pointy ears—suggest he's from the same species as Yoda, the legendary Jedi Master who trained countless generations of Jedi Knights before the rise of the Empire. At this point, very little is known about this particular species, including its name or home planet; however, its members appear to have a centuries-long lifespan and they appear to age very slowly.

2 /

1 / All known members of the Child's species appear to have a strong connection to the Force.

2 / The moment the Mandalorian realizes that the fifty-year-old asset he was looking for is actually an infant.

After being brought to the Client's outpost on planet Nevarro, the Child was sedated and analyzed. But before any harm was done to him, he was rescued by the Mandalorian, who felt remorseful and had a sudden change of heart. Together with the bounty hunter, the Child started to travel across space and eventually returned to Nevarro. Captured by two Imperial scout troopers, who treated him badly, the little creature was then saved by the reprogrammed IG-11 and returned to Mando. Now the Child is officially a Mandalorian foundling and forms a clan of two with his protector.

4 /

TRULY WONDERFUL

Though very young, the Child has proven to be extremely sensitive to the Force—an energy field that flows through all living things which can grant special abilities to those who are able to harness its power. While fighting a huge mudhorn on Arvala-7, the Mandalorian first witnessed the Child's connection to this mysterious energy: The tiny creature used the Force to telekinetically immobilize the enraged beast, thus saving the gunfighter from certain death.

His abilities are at an early stage, but the Child can also use his power to move surprisingly fast, to block and redirect energy, such as a stream of fire shot by a flamethrower, and to heal mortal wounds. To a certain extent, the Child is aware of these abilities and often employs them to help his friends. However, when performed, these Force-related abilities also seem to wear him out.

3 / The Child wrapped in a blanket inside his floating crib.

4 / With a special device, Dr. Pershing and the Client check the Child's health conditions.

5 / At such a young age, the Child is still learning to master his overwhelming Force abilities.

6 / Using the Force, the Child manages to save the Mandalorian from a huge mudhorn.

5 /

6 /

7 / From the moment he sets his eyes on him, the Mandalorian immediately connects with the Child.

AN ADORABLE WOMP RAT

Aside from the powers which make him quite special, the Child acts and behaves like any infant would. He loves to wander around and play—especially when coming across tasty frogs he can snack on. He also likes to push random buttons on the *Razor Crest*—an activity that he excels at independently of the Force and that doesn't really meet the Mandalorian's approval. Also, like many of his peers, he never does as he's told, often coming out of hiding when he isn't supposed to.

The Child may be tiny in size, but his heart is as big as a mudhorn. Deeply grateful to the Mandalorian for having rescued him, the critter develops a strong affection for the gunfighter, whom he considers a sort of heavily-armed father. For this reason, the Child often tries to protect him using his powers, sometimes taking it too far—like that time he mistook an arm-wrestling match for a real fight and almost strangled the Mandalorian's ally and friend Cara Dune.

BEHIND THE SCENES

Brought to the screen by a combination of methods, the Child is sometimes an intricate puppet, sometimes a computer generated character realized by ILM (Industrial Light & Magic), and sometimes a both. The process to create the Child started with a line from the script that just describes him as a baby of the same race as Yoda. Dave Filoni first sketched a little drawing of the Mandalorian in front of an egg-shaped floating pram from which a hand raises: that drawing became the starting point for design supervisor Doug Chiang and the art department. According to Jon Favreau, the hardest part was working on the big eyes and the moving ears, since the expressions and the emotion of the character don't come from the face but from those two elements combined. "We got lots and lots of drawings," said the executive producer, "some of them were too cute, some too ugly, some of them were the wrong proportions." Finally, an image

8 / Despite his great powers, the Child is still a defenseless being in need of the Mandalorian's protection.

9 / Flying away with his jetpack, the Mandalorian brings the Child to safety —the same way he was rescued as a boy by a Mandalorian.

10 / A technician at work on the Child's floating crib.

11 /

11 / The Child's eyes, ears, mouth, head and body were operated by several puppeteers at the same time.

12 / Director Deborah Chow holding the Child on set.

13 / The Child's puppeteers on set.

12 /

realized by concept artist Christian Alzmann, which showed the Child wrapped up in a flight jacket, was charming enough to make the producers say "this is good." They had found it. The design of the tiny creature developed from there. Based on Alzmann's concept art, the creature was then brought to screen by special effects studio Legacy Effects, who spent around three months building it. Once on stage, the Child was operated by a team of puppeteers, each of them controlling a specific body part at the same time. As Jason Matthews of Legacy Effects says: "It's just like the band jamming, how you start to get into a rhythm, and you know when the head is going to turn left, and I'll try to beat it, leading with the eyes... it starts to work itself out." According to actress Gina Carano (who plays Cara Dune), working with the puppet proved to be quite challenging as the Child would always steal the actors' thunder: "If you're in a scene with that little baby, you're completely going to lose the scene, no matter what." ⚔

GREEF KARGA

former disgraced magistrate, now an agent of the Bounty Hunters Guild, Greef Karga is the person any hunter turns to when they are looking for a bounty. Shrewd, wise, and charismatic, Karga always follows the Guild protocols and doesn't tolerate those who break the bounty hunting rules. Despite looking out first and foremost for his own interests, he is not devoid of conscience and knows how to show gratitude.

THE GUILD

Bounty hunters travel across the galaxy looking for fugitives, criminals, outlaws, and anyone with a bounty on their head. Once the prey is captured, sometimes dead, sometimes alive, the hunters deliver it to the agent who gave them the assignment, in return for a payment. The Guild, and the agent, get a commission off the bounty—this is why Greef Karga

is always happy to see the Mandalorian, one of the most efficient, if not *the* most efficient hunter he works with. However, many clients don't want to pay Guild rates and make private arrangements, putting at risk the very hunters they hire. In fact, the Guild members must follow a code: they cannot kill another hunter or interfere with another's hunt. Outside the Guild, anything can happen. When the hunters accept the job, they receive a bounty puck, a small device that contains all the information they need, including a holographic image of their target. Another device, a short range tracking fob, is locked to the quarry's biological signal and leads the hunters to their prey. Each member of the Guild that had a tracking fob locked to the Child's signal could find him. This threat made the Mandalorian accept Greef Karga's offer to go back to Nevarro, kill the Client and free the city in exchange for having his name cleared with the Guild and the tracking fobs deactivated.

2 /

3 /

A MAN OF HONOR

1 / As an agent of the Guild, Greef Karga acts as the middleman in the talks between bounty hunters and clients. (See previous spread)

2 / Karga hands out tracking fobs to the Guild's hunters to help them locate bounties. (See previous spread)

3 / Initially unconcerned with protecting the Child, Karga soon changed his mind.

4 / Karga and Dune bid farewell to the Mandalorian and the Child.

5 / In order to get the Child back, Karga is willing to double-cross the Mandalorian and his allies.

Greef Karga trusted the Mandalorian and considered him a man of honor. The bounty hunter always captured his prey, guaranteeing him a good profit. However, when the Mandalorian broke the rules and betrayed the Guild, Karga didn't hesitate to gather members of the Guild to keep him from leaving the planet with the Child. To the agent, the little being was just a delivered bounty, and Mando was just a traitor. Saved by his tribe, Mando managed to reach his ship, but Karga was already there. "I didn't want it to come to this," he said to the hunter, "but then you broke the Code." Greef shot but missed. Mando didn't. A direct shot to the heart that, luckily for Greef, hit the beskar he pocketed, ironically, as a commission from the bounty of the Child himself. Later, Karga planned to lure Mando back to Nevarro, under the guise of getting rid of the Imperials, kill him and take the Child. But after the Child healed him from a mortal wound, the agent changed his mind. Impressed by his power and generosity, Karga joined the Mandalorian and his team, thus helping him and the Child escape Moff Gideon, and at the same time, liberate his city. In the end, Greef Karga realized he is a man of honor as well.

4 /

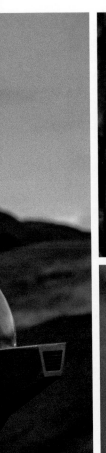

7 /

WISE GUN

Despite spending most of his time collecting tracking fobs, giving pucks to hunters, or trying to pay them with old Imperial credits—a currency that doesn't have much value anymore—Greef Karga is also a skilled fighter, not only because of his ability to shoot with two blaster pistols at the same time but because he always reflects before shooting, selecting the best target instead of the most obvious. When the Mandalorian tried to get away with the Child aboard a speeder, he could have made it if it wasn't for Greef: the agent shot the droid driving the speeder, breaking off the escape.

6 / When the situation calls for it, Karga can also count on good shooting skills.

7 / Attacked by reptavians, Karga was promptly saved by the Child who used the Force to heal his wounds.

BEHIND THE SCENES

In the very beginning, Carl Weathers agreed to play Greef Karga because he wanted to work with Jon Favreau and the production team. But, as a professional, he needed to read the script first. "As an actor," he explained, "you're somehow endorsing what someone wants to say about the world or in the world." And when he finally did read the script, Carl realized it was perfect. And he was in.

A legend who played Apollo Creed in four *Rocky* films, a "superstar"—as actress Gina Carano (Cara Dune) called him—Carl Weathers wasn't supposed to be in the whole show. His character should have died in episode 3 when he was shot by the Mandalorian. He was also supposed to be a Weequay character, wearing full prosthetic makeup. But then, executive producers Jon Favreau and Dave Filoni realized they really couldn't cover his face. Weathers agreed: "People are gonna tune in if you got the name. Why not have the face?" So he was spared an early demise and an alien background, becoming one of the most important characters of *The Mandalorian*.

"There's something about this character," explained the actor, "that reminds me of a combination of John Huston and Orson Welles. There is this largesse about him, there is this commanding sort of presence about him that he doesn't try to do, but that's just who is. When he walks into a space, not a room, any space, he fills that space." Through Weathers' performance, Karga went from being just a bad guy, an antagonist with no redemption, to an all-round character who represents the flaws of all human beings that can lead to the dark side. In the words of the actor: "The story of Greef is that he is tempted." ☥

8 / Pedro Pascal, Carl Weathers and Gina Carano on set. Carano found Weathers particularly inspirational for his ability to "command presence."

9 / Karga pretends to turn the Mandalorian and Dune in.

10 / Actor Carl Weathers strove to depict Karga as a very human character with both strengths and weaknesses.

THE CLIENT & DOCTOR PERSHING

Though it may look they have a lot in common—both are former Imperial officers and still work for Moff Gideon, even if the Empire is no more—"the Client" and Doctor Pershing are very different at heart. They are both after the Child, but unlike the scientist, the Client would do anything in his power to obtain the tiny creature. Even if that means hiring someone to, as the Mandalorian would say, "bring him in cold"…

IMPERIAL NOSTALGIA

The Client's name and past may be shrouded in secrecy, but the Imperial emblem on the medallion around his neck leaves no doubt about his political affiliation. Cold-hearted and shadowy, the Client works for a remnant of the late Galactic Empire, which he still considers the only form of government worth pursuing. For this reason, the Client has a strong aversion to those who resisted the Imperial expansion and disrupted the "natural order of things" that led to its collapse. With his silver hair, cold eyes and refined manner of speaking, the Client has a somewhat intimidating appearance—to such an extent that even the undaunted Greef Karga behaves quite cautiously when dealing with him.

1 /

1 / The Client reports to ruthless Moff Gideon, leader of an Imperial remnant.

2 / Armor worn by the Client's stormtroopers appears to be rather dirty and worn-out.

3 / All the Client cares about is retrieving an unspecified "asset" by all necessary means.

2 /

4 /

A LIFE FOR A LIFE

By contrast, Doctor Pershing seems a rather fearful man—especially when in the presence of weapons and alert Mandalorians. Together with the Client, the young scientist was tasked by Moff Gideon with the Child's retrieval. When meeting Mando to discuss the terms of the bounty placed on the creature, Pershing timidly specified that the infant had to be delivered alive. The Client, however, immediately rectified such request, explaining that "proof of termination" would also be acceptable "for a lower fee".

Upon delivery of the asset, Pershing left the room and took the Child with him. He was then urged by the Client to "extract the necessary material" from the creature by all means necessary. The scientist, however, refused to do so, reiterating that they had received specific instructions to bring the Child back alive. Little did he know that such stubbornness would ultimately grant his safety. When the Mandalorian went back to rescue the Child from the Imperial facility, he realized that Pershing was the only one trying to protect him, and therefore decided to spare his life.

BEHIND THE SCENES

The unnamed character known as "the Client" is played by a famous film director: Werner Herzog. Once described by François Truffaut as "the most important film director alive," Herzog has worked on over 60 movies throughout his career and in 1982, he won the Best Director award at Cannes Film Festival. Despite having no former knowledge of the *Star Wars* saga, Herzog was immediately intrigued by the series' screenplay and storytelling. He especially grew fond of 'The Child' puppet, which he described as "heartbreakingly beautiful." As reported by director Deborah Chow, while shooting the third episode Herzog "got so into it that he started directing the baby as though as he was talking to a person."

5 /

4 / Dr. Pershing seems to be the only Imperial concerned with the Child's safety.

5 / Actor and film director Werner Herzog as the Imperial officer whose name is never revealed, in this on-set shot.

6 / Dr. Pershing (Omid Abtahi) and the Client (Werner Herzog) check the Child in this behind--the-scenes shot.

7 / Behind-the-scenes shot with Chapter 3 director Deborah Chow and actor Werner Herzog.

7 /

KUIIL

A former slave under the Galactic Empire, Kuiil has earned his own freedom by the sweat of his thick, white brow. He treasures the tranquility he has found on planet Arvala-7, but peace, just like freedom, comes at a price. Despite having spent many years in solitude, Kuiil is, in his own way, generous and kind—though it's better not to argue with him once he "has spoken."

SEEKING PEACE

After buying his freedom through hard work and labor, Kuiil settled on planet Arvala-7, where he accomplished what he was seeking most: serving no one but himself. For many years, working in a vapor farm with just his blurrgs for company, the Ugnaught lived a quiet life. However, when bounty hunters started to comb the area in search of the Child, the situation changed drastically. The valley chosen by Kuiil as his forever home had become "an endless stream of mercenaries bringing destruction." Believing that the sooner they found the creature, the sooner they would leave once and for all, Kuiil then started to help hunters with their mission. Unfortunately, they would all die in the attempt—all, but one: a certain Mandalorian coming from Nevarro...

1 /

1 / Kuiil found his well-earned peace on planet Arvala-7.

2 / Kuiil is an Ugnaught, a species whose members were often employed as servants under the Galactic Empire.

3 / Thanks to his skills, Kuiil is self-reliant and lives completely off the grid.

4 / After being reprogrammed, droid IG-11 became a useful assistant to Kuiil.

5 / Misty Rosas (Kuiil), Pedro Pascal, and Gina Carano shoot the blurrg riding scenes.

6 / Kuiil's animatronic face mask worn by Misty Rosas; its eyebrows and mouth were controlled by puppeteers.

A KIND-HEARTED JACK OF ALL TRADES

From blurrg breeding to droid repair, old Kuiil has developed a wide variety of skills over his lifetime. Not only did he help the Mandalorian negotiate with Jawas after they had stripped the *Razor Crest*, but he also contributed to its repair once Djarin got the looted parts back. A talented mechanic, Kuiil also managed to reconstruct droid IG-11, which was blasted by the Mandalorian upon rescuing the Child, as well as to reprogramme it for nursing, much to the Mandalorian's dismay. However, Kuiil's greatest skills lie in his heart rather than his hands. He willingly helped the Mandalorian protect the Child from Imperial slavery, an action which cost him his life.

BEHIND THE SCENES

As a homage to die-hard fans, series creators endeavored to feature minor characters or races from the *Star Wars* saga. This is the case with Ugnaughts, the relatively unknown species Kuiil belongs to. Bringing Kuiil to life required a combination of performance, puppetry and animatronics. While filming, performance artist Misty Rosas wore an animatronic face mask which was additionally controlled by puppeteers. As explained by Rosas herself, there would be a puppeteer operating the character's mouth "and another puppeteer working in doing the eyebrows." According to Rosas, shooting Kuiil's scenes proved particularly challenging as puppeteers couldn't hear her; to make them get the timing right, the actress strived to give them physical cues. Ultimately, actor Nick Nolte was chosen to perform Kuiil's voice. ⚜

6 /

IG-11

With his crimson sensors and powerful blasters, droid IG-11 may look really intimidating, but as a wise Ugnaught once said, droids merely reflect those who imprint them, and IG-11 is no exception. Formerly a ruthless bounty hunter, then a protective nurse with outstanding tea-making skills, the slim gunfighter proves to be a loyal and trusted ally—to such an extent that even the Mandalorian has to put his aversion to droids aside…

A FELLOW BOUNTY HUNTER

Just like the Mandalorian, assassin droid IG-11 is a bounty hunter. Thanks to his double-jointed shoulders and elbows, he is extremely agile and can fight multiple targets simultaneously. On top of this, he is incredibly fast and is able to rotate his torso and head 360 degrees. Relentless and determined, IG-11 is programmed to adhere to the Guild protocols, as well as to initiate a self-destruct sequence to avoid being captured by enemies.

Commissioned to hunt down the very same asset, IG-11 and Mando met at the mercenary encampment on Arvala-7. Upon learning they were both on assignment, they decided to join forces and split the mission's reward—although IG-11 claimed for himself the "reputation merits" associated with it. Once in front of the Child's floating pram, however, the pair realized they had different ideas about what to do with him. Indeed, the Mandalorian wanted to deliver the infant alive, whereas IG-11 had received instructions to terminate him. Before he could shoot the Child, the Mandalorian gunned down the droid, switching off his sensors forever… or perhaps not.

2 /

1 / IG-11's design was inspired by IG-88, a minor character from *The Empire Strikes Back*.

2 / IG-11's revolvable head and torso allowed him to handle multiple enemies at the same time.

3 /

4 /

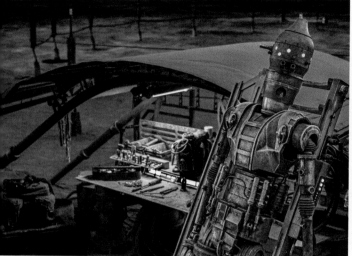

5 /

A NEW LIFE, A NEW BASE FUNCTION

3 / After being shot by the Mandalorian, IG-11 was fully reconstructed by Kuiil.

4 / IG-11 was equipped with a built-in detonator which could activate a self-destruct mechanism.

5 / IG-11 saves the Child from the Nevarro scout troopers.

Some time later, IG-11's flotsam, still lying in the mercenary encampment, is retrieved by Kuiil, who takes it back to his farm. There, the Ugnaught started to work on the droid's reconstruction—a process which proved to be, in Kuiil's own words, "quite difficult, but not impossible." Due to its heavily damaged neural harness, IG-11 had to learn everything from scratch. While gaining further experience, he developed a personality of his own, and became a helpful and polite assistant to the farmer.

When Mando later attempted to hire Kuiil's services to protect the Child from Moff Gideon and his Imperials, he offered to reprogram the droid for nursing and protocol instead, a decision to which Mando reluctantly agreed. IG-11 thus became a nurse droid. Despite Mando's mistrust, the droid amazingly served his purpose. In fact, not only did he rescue the Child from a pair of scout troopers, but he also managed to save the Mandalorian's life by healing his mortal wounds with bacta spray.

In what would become his final battle, IG-11 sacrificed himself for the greater good of his friends. By activating his self-destruct sequence to kill a platoon of stormtroopers, the nurse droid saved the Child, the Mandalorian, Karga, and Dune—thus fulfilling his base function for the last time.

6 /

6 / A physical puppet
was used in close-ups
and medium-shots.

7 / Due to its
development in the
story, IG-11 had to
be portrayed as a
rather unthreatening
character.

8 / Producers Dave
Filoni and Jon Favreau
examine the IG-11
puppet in action.

9 / IG-11 poses with
director Taika Waititi,
who lent him his voice.

8 /

7 /

BEHIND THE SCENES

IG-11's concept design was based upon that of IG-88,
an assassin droid which first appeared in *The Empire
Strikes Back* and looked, as commented by Filoni,
"amazingly cool."

According to the original brief sent to the visual
effects team, IG-11 needed to look like an assembly
of old and heavy car parts. His joints had to be
animated as if they were loosely fitted together to
give him a somewhat awkward look. As explained
by Animation Director Hal Hickel, the droid was
eventually brought to life through a combination
of motion capture and animation, as well as by
building a physical puppet for close-ups and
medium shots.

IG-11 is voiced by the season finale's director: Taika
Waititi. According to Waititi, the main challenge was
to find the right balance in conveying the personality
of a non-living, seemingly unemotional character. ⚓

9 /

CARASYNTHIA "CARA" DUNE

Fierce and gritty, Cara Dune is—by all means—a woman of action. A skillful warrior, Cara served as a shock trooper in the Galactic Civil War. Now she makes a living as a mercenary and tries to lay low, at least until someone is up for a fight. Though no longer "in the mood to play soldier," Dune is ready to dust off her skills if the enemy turns out to be an Imperial…

AN EARLY RETIREMENT

Like the Mando, Cara Dune is anything but an open book; yet, the tattoo under her left eye— a Rebel Alliance Starbird—leaves no doubt about her political affiliation.

Cara Dune was born on Alderaan, a planet which was utterly destroyed by the massive Imperial weapon known as the Death Star. Enlisting in the Rebellion's army, Dune fought as a shock trooper during the Galactic Civil War. After the Rebels' victory, however, Dune left the Alliance. Her role under the New Republic was closer to that of a "peacekeeper" rather than a soldier, something she "didn't sign up for." Dune then started working as a mercenary—a business that by definition entails an array of activities, many of which would "carry a life sentence." For this reason, Dune started to travel across the Outer Rim Territories, finding a suitable hideout on planet Sorgan. Even though the Empire seems to be gone for good, her hatred is still very much alive. For this reason, when the Mandalorian offers her to join him in his mission against an alleged Imperial remnant, she doesn't need to think twice.

1 /

1 / Cara Dune and Mando part ways without knowing that their paths will cross again very soon. (See previous spread)

2 / Mercenary Cara Dune travels across space in search of suitable planets where to lay low. (See previous spread)

3 / A former shock trooper, Cara Dune has a Rebel Alliance Starbird tattoo on her left cheek.

4 / Dune channels her fury against Imperials.

STRONG INSIDE AND OUT

As the Mandalorian has experienced first-hand, Cara Dune has exceptional fighting skills, especially when it comes to hand-to-hand combat. Due to her past in the army, the war veteran is also a skilful military tactician. When hired, together with Mando, by Sorgan villagers to help them defeat a group of raiders, Dune laid out a plan which proved to be highly effective. But Dune's strength goes way beyond her physical capabilities. A brave and determined woman, she always stands up for what she believes in—an attitude which, along with her skills, will grant her an offer to become Greef Karga's enforcer. Though a bit of a loner, Dune becomes attached to the Mandalorian, who quickly becomes her favorite arm-wrestling competitor. She even bonds with the Child —despite his attempt to strangle her with his powers.

3 /

4 /

5 /

6 /

BEHIND THE SCENES

A former MMA (Mixed Martial Arts) fighter, Gina Carano doesn't feel like the regular, Hollywood actress; as such, she immediately connected with fierce and unconventional Cara Dune. Due to her background as a professional fighter, Carano often performs her own stunts. As commented by Favreau, "Gina lights up when she is doing the action stuff… you can tell she loves being that character in this world." The producer and director also praised her authenticity during the fight scenes, comparing "the way she takes a hit" to that of Harrison Ford in the *Indiana Jones* films.

Dune's costume, created by Brian Matyas and Joseph Porro, was designed to highlight the character's stamina while conveying a sense of femininity at the same time. As further explained by director Bryce Dallas Howard, Dune's silhouette had to be immediately recognizable, in line with all iconic characters from the *Star Wars* saga. ⚓

7 /

5 / Thanks to her previous career as an MMA fighter, Carano could perform the majority of her own stunts.

6 / Armwrestling partners Carano and Pascal smile for the camera.

7 / Carano and director Taika Waititi on set.

THE ARMORER

The Mandalorian known as the Armorer is the covert's gatekeeper and wisest member. A calm yet authoritative warrior, she resides in the heart of the covert, where she forges weapons and armor for the whole clan. Profoundly devoted to the Mandalorian's creed, the Armorer provides guidance to those who walk the same path—for, as she would say, "This is the Way."

WARRIOR IN FUR

Just like the hammer that forges iron, the Armorer moulds and strengthens the sense of belonging of fellow Mandalorians. Poised and collected, the Armorer rarely speaks, nor does she ever raise her voice; yet, her undisputed authority is acknowledged by all clan members, regardless of their rank or exploits. A skilled blacksmith, the Armorer often crafts and repairs gear for other Mandalorians. When Mando returned to the enclave with the reward beskar obtained by the Client, the Armorer forged him a full cuirass, pauldrons, and weapons. Welcoming his request, she also reserved some metal for the Foundlings, whom she refers to as the future of their kind. The Armorer is strongly committed to the tribe's code of conduct and values, which she defines as "the Way of the Mandalore." However, she's also aware that tensions between fellow Mandalorians may arise—especially after the Imperial persecution which forced them to hide and live in the shadows. During a quarrel between Mando and Paz Vizsla, a heavy infantry Mandalorian who accused Mando of cowardice for sharing tables with Imperials, she stepped in to defuse the fight, offering a reminder that Mando had never violated any of the tribe's rules. The Armorer also explained that those who walk the Way of the Mandalore are both hunter and prey. As such, no Imperial sympathizer would ever choose the Mandalorians' way of life. Later, the covert was discovered by Moff Gideon's Imperial remnant, who ruthlessly murdered almost all of its members. Instead of fleeing, the Armorer decided to stay and salvage any remaining beskar, thus further demonstrating her devotion to the Creed. Shortly after, while helping Mando and the Child escape from Gideon's soldiers, she declared them a newly-formed clan of two. Before parting ways, she commissioned the Mandalorian to reunite the Child to its own kind, as per the Way's code of conduct. As a Mandalorian, the Armorer sure knows how to fight—as demonstrated by her being able to knock out five stormtroopers with just a forging hammer and tongs.

1 / The Armorer checks the reward beskar steel provided by Mando. (See previous spread)

2 / The Armorer holding her hammer and tongs in front of the forge. (See previous spread)

BEHIND THE SCENES

The Armorer is portrayed by actress Emily Swallow, while the stunts are performed by Lauren Mary Kim (who also worked as stunt double for Julia Jones, the actress who plays Omera in Chapter 4). According to Swallow, the costume, which included a Spartan-like helmet and thick welding gloves, proved particularly difficult to wear while shooting. The helmet provided no peripheral vision, while the gloves made it actually difficult to pick things up. However, there also was a bright side to it, namely the fact that Swallow didn't have to wear any makeup: "It's ridiculous, but that was one part that I got so excited about, because normally I have to get to set like two hours before I shoot to go through hair and makeup." According to the actress, director Deborah Chow was a great inspiration for such personality traits: "She commands authority without any effort… she draws you in, and I recognized that that could be useful to the Armorer."

3 /

4 /

5 /

3 / Jon Favreau and Taika Waititi pay a visit to the Armorer's Forge.

4 / Emily Swallow removing the Armorer's spiked helmet.

5 / Pre-production shot featuring several designs of Mandalorian helmets.

6 / Favreau and Swallow hold the Armorer's tools.

7 / According to Emily Swallow, one of the perks of playing the Armorer was that she didn't need to wear makeup on set.

7 /

SEASON ONE GUIDE | 61

MOFF GIDEON

A powerful warlord at the helm of an Imperial remnant, Moff Gideon has only one purpose: to seize the being known as the Child. Ruthless with enemies and allies alike, Gideon instils fear into most of the troopers and officers in his service. He will stop at nothing to obtain what he wants, even if that means crushing anyone in his path.

RISING FROM IMPERIAL ASHES

Under the Galactic Empire, Gideon served as an officer in the intelligence organization known as the Imperial Security Bureau. During that time, he also participated in the Great Purge, a conflict which led to many Mandalorians getting killed. He was eventually appointed as "Moff"—a rank designating governors in charge of specific galactic sectors for the Empire. With the rise of the New Republic, Moff Gideon managed to stage his death and get away safely in the Outer Rim Territories. He became the leader of an Imperial remnant operating around Nevarro.

A RUTHLESS IMP

Clever and determined, Gideon is willing to do anything in his power to obtain the Child. His experience as an Imperial officer has made him a rather good strategist who's always a step ahead of his opponents. The Moff also proved to be merciless towards anyone he has no use for. In fact, he didn't hesitate to kill the Client, despite him being one of his most faithful allies.

1/

1 / As the elite soldiers of Imperial Military Intelligence, death troopers are provided with advanced armor and gear. (See previous spread)

A LEGENDARY ARTIFACT

Unbeknownst to Mando, Karga and Dune, Moff Gideon still lives. Indeed, the Imperial didn't die in the crash of his TIE fighter—destroyed by the Mandalorian in an aerial duel. Trapped inside the ship's wrecked hull, Gideon freed himself wielding a mysterious weapon known as the Darksaber. This unique, dark-energy blade is well-known by Mandalorians, as it was created by one of their own: Tarre Vizsla, the first Mandalorian warrior to ever become a Jedi Knight. For centuries, the Darksaber became a symbol of power to Mandalorians, for they would follow the warrior controlling it. Whilst it is unknown how the Darksaber ended up in an Imperial's gloved hands, the fact that Moff Gideon wields such a powerful weapon doesn't bode well for Mando and his allies…

4 /

5 /

2 / As a former Imperial Security Bureau officer, Gideon is amongst the few people who know the Mandalorian's real name. (See previous spread)

3 / Merciless Gideon can also be quite short-tempered: indeed, he kills one of his own men for interrupting him.

4 / The Mandalorian uses his grappling cable to reach Gideon's TIE fighter.

5 / Gideon loses control of the ship after the Mandalorian placed a detonator on the TIE fighter's left wing pylon.

BEHIND THE SCENES

Moff Gideon is portrayed by Giancarlo Esposito. The actor considers the original saga an essential part of his childhood, for those movies gave him "the ability to dream."

Esposito doesn't regard Moff Gideon as a villain and argued that it's impossible to frame him as a good or evil character. In fact, he described the Imperial officer as a rather complex character and claimed that such complicated nature was what fascinated him the most.

Despite not having any screen time together, Esposito grew fond of the Child. He particularly enjoyed the combination of "child-like wonder" and "adult intelligence" conveyed by the puppet's eyes. He also very much enjoyed shooting inside the Volume —a wraparound LED screen showing computer generated images of the backgrounds that surrounded a physical set and the actors. According to Esposito this photo-real, practical set was much better than the usual green-screen technology because it helped actors to complete the environment. "It's like we've put them inside a video game," said Kim Libreri— chief technical officer of Epic Games who collaborated with the show. "The fact that we're able to go to these locations, I think they got better content, better performances. It's like going back to the days when George [Lucas] was out there in Tunisia. It feels like classic *Star Wars*... and it's going to have resonance for many years."

6 / Gideon's costume was conceived by concept artist Brian Matyas.

7 / Carano, Filoni, Pascal, and Weathers pose with Gideon's stormtroopers. Due to the lack of available stormtrooper costumes on set, Favreau and Filoni sought the help of a local fan organization.

8 / The actors inside the wraparound screen technology known as the Volume, which Giancarlo Esposito particularly enjoyed.

6 /

HUNTERS AND PREY

Whether friends or enemies, strangers or estranged, the Mandalorian has many encounters as he makes his way through the galaxy.

1 / Heavy infantry Mandalorian Paz Vizsla accuses Mando of taking jobs from the Empire. (See previous spread)

PAZ VIZSLA

Paz Vizsla is a heavy infantry Mandalorian operating on Nevarro. Initially upset with Mando for "sharing tables" and doing business with the Empire, he eventually helps him protect the Child from several bounty hunters and Greef Karga, in accordance with the Way of the Mandalore. Very strong and skilled in combat, Vizsla wears heavy Mandalorian armor and wields a blaster cannon.

3 /

OFFWORLD JAWAS

With its endless deserts and craggy ravines, Arvala-7 is the perfect place for Jawas to prosper. Obsessed with technology just like their Tatooine counterparts, the band of Jawas living on Arvala-7 are always on the hunt for equipment and ship or droid parts they can steal and resell. Along with their passion for scavenging, Jawas are also fond of mudhorn eggs, which they consider an exquisite delicacy.

2 / This is the way: Paz Vizsla and fellow Mandalorians join Din Djarin in battle

3 / A group of Jawas peeking through their rough cloth capes.

4 / Jawas are always on the alert —especially after stealing one's ship parts.

4 /

6 /

TORO CALICAN

Toro Calican was a young and inexperienced bounty hunter eager to join the Guild. On a quest to track down assassin Fennec Shand, Calican teamed up with Mando to maximise the chances of success. However, his thirst for glory made him venture too far and betray the Mandalorian—a foolish endeavor which cost the hunter his young life.

5 /

5 / The way Toro lounged when he first met Mando resembles Han Solo's first scene in Episode IV.

6 / Mando and Calican hunt down Fennec Shand using speeder bikes on Tatooine.

PELI MOTTO

Peli Motto runs a hangar at Mos Eisley spaceport on Tatooine. A surly mechanic, Motto has no time to waste—for time, as every Mos Eisley regular knows, is money. For this reason, she's more than happy to repair Mando's ship—and to charge him extra for looking after the Child. Motto can be found at Bay 3-5, either working or playing sabacc with her droid assistants.

7 / Though she would never admit it, Peli Motto didn't mind looking after the Child.

8 / Mechanic Peli Motto runs the Bay 3-5 hangar on Tatooine.

9 /

9 / Elite mercenary Fennec Shand is portrayed by actress Ming-Na Wen.

10 / Shand using her MK-modified rifle against Mando and Calican.

11 / Mayfeld, Burg, Qin, and Xi'an realize the Mandalorian has escaped from captivity!

12 / Q9-0 is destroyed by Mando before he can kill the Child.

13 / The criminal and bandit known as Ran Malk.

10 /

FENNEC SHAND

Her great fighting skills, combined with a sharp mind, made Fennec Shand one of the most renowned assassins in the galaxy. An elite mercenary with an impressive client portfolio, Shand was eventually captured by Mando and Calican. In a last attempt to save herself, Shand offered Calican to join forces and catch the Mandalorian instead—but who would trust an assassin with such a reputation?

RANZAR "RAN" MALK AND HIS GANG

An old acquaintance of Mando, Ranzar "Ran" Malk was a bandit who operated on a space station in the Outer Rim Territories. The two used to work together back in the "good old days", but eventually parted ways. When Mando reached out to his former partner looking for jobs, Malk suggested he join a team of mercenaries about to rescue an alleged associate from a prison ship. The gang included ex-Imperial sharpshooter Mayfeld, meticulous protocol droid Q9-0, muscular Devaronian Burg, and Xi'an, a Twi'lek mercenary with whom the Mandalorian was reputed to have had an affair. Upon reaching the New Republic prison ship, the bounty hunter discovered that the gang was actually rescuing Qin—Xi'an's brother and definitely not Mando's biggest fan…

14 / Widow Omera
hugging her daughter
Winta after raiders
attacked their village.

15 / Sorgan krill
farmers are adamant
about not leaving their
village.

16 / Cara Dune and
Mando enjoy the
peace and quiet of
Sorgan with farmer
Omera.

17 / For a moment,
Mando thinks a life
among the farmers
could be possible.

SORGAN VILLAGERS

Sorgan is home to a group of krill farmers who live in a village near the planet's ponds. Peaceful and friendly, the farmers live a frugal and simple life surrounded by nature. While fighting some raiders with the help of Mando and Dune, some of them, however, showed unexpected combat skills—such as widow Omera, who proved to be a proficient sharpshooter.

14 /

15 /

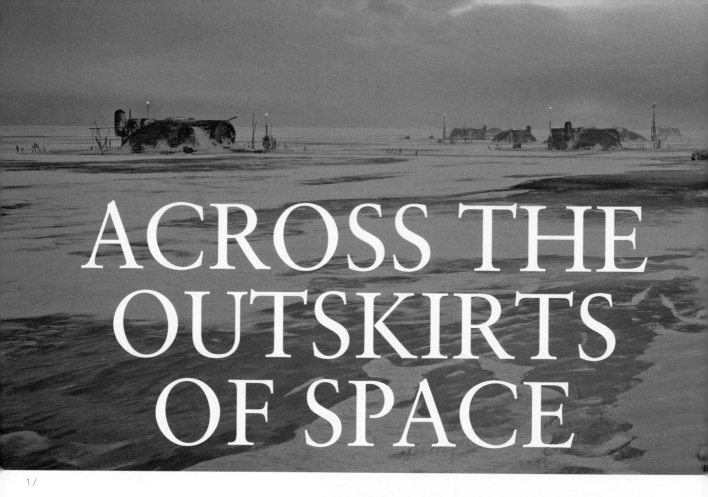

ACROSS THE OUTSKIRTS OF SPACE

1 /

F rom freezing landscapes buried under ice and snow to boggy and thick forests, up to arid deserts almost devoid of vegetation, a bounty hunter must be prepared for any possible scenario—especially when such worlds are far away from justice and law.

ICE PLANET

With its freezing winds and hostile environment, this ice planet probably isn't the most coveted location in the galaxy. The planet is home to an indigenous species known as the ravinak—a gigantic, tusked creature which hides underneath the ice. Ravinaks are quite aggressive and often attack their prey by emerging from the ice and dragging them underwater.

NEVARRO

Ruled by the Empire until the very end of the Galactic Civil War, Nevarro is a planet inhabited by several species and races. Far from the New Republic's control, it is the perfect place for outlaws and bounty hunters to conduct their business. Indeed, the local common house is often visited by Guild members and Greef Karga himself. Nevarro was also home to a Mandalorian covert which was later discovered and attacked by Moff Gideon's soldiers.

1 / Intrepid travelers who end up on this ice planet can find shelter inside this settlement's public house.

2 / On his way to Greef Karga, the Mandalorian meets a Jawa at the local market of Nevarro.

2 /

3 / Jawas use sandcrawlers to move across the desert lands of Arvala-7 and transport the parts they scavenge.

ARVALA-7

Before being constantly visited by bounty hunters, Arvala-7 was a world mainly inhabited by those who were seeking a peaceful life. The planet's desert lands are home to several creatures such as blurrgs and mudhorns, as well as to the mercenary encampment where the Child was first located. Jawas can also be spotted diving through the sandy dunes aboard their sandcrawler.

SORGAN

With no starports or industrial centers, and very little population density, forest planet Sorgan makes a good hideout for those who need to lay low, which is why both Mando and Cara Dune ended up there. Mainly inhabited by krill farmers, the swamp planet is also home to tiny, one-eyed frogs which appear to be the Child's favorite meal.

TATOOINE

A very wise Jedi once said that it's impossible to find "a more wretched hive of scum and villainy" than Mos Eisley spaceport on Tatooine. Indeed, the desert planet has a reputation for being an utterly lawless world full of smugglers and criminals. Orbiting two suns, Tatooine has an arid climate; luckily, the local cantina offers several beverages to soothe one's thirst—as well as lots of dimly-lit corners where to do business.

4 /

5 /

4 / A view of Sorgan's forested surface from space.

5 / Mando enters Mos Eisley spaceport on Tatooine. The planet was the former home of famous Jedi Master Luke Skywalker.

MOVING THE

1 / The *Razor Crest* is also the closest thing to a home for the Mandalorian.

GALAXY

W hether on land or in space, means of transports are pivotal for traveling across the galaxy. From pre-Empire classics to specially modified crafts, an efficient means of transport can truly make the difference both on and off the battlefield.

RAZOR CREST

Originally a military spacecraft used for patrol duties, the *Razor Crest* is, by all means, the Mandalorian's most trusted ally. With its leaking power lines and partially-efficient hyperdrive, the ship is far from being in mint condition: yet, as a pre-Empire craft, the *Razor Crest* is entirely "off the grid," a feature which proves extremely useful when hunting down bounties. Equipped with two laser cannons, the ship also comes with a control lever for the Child to enjoy.

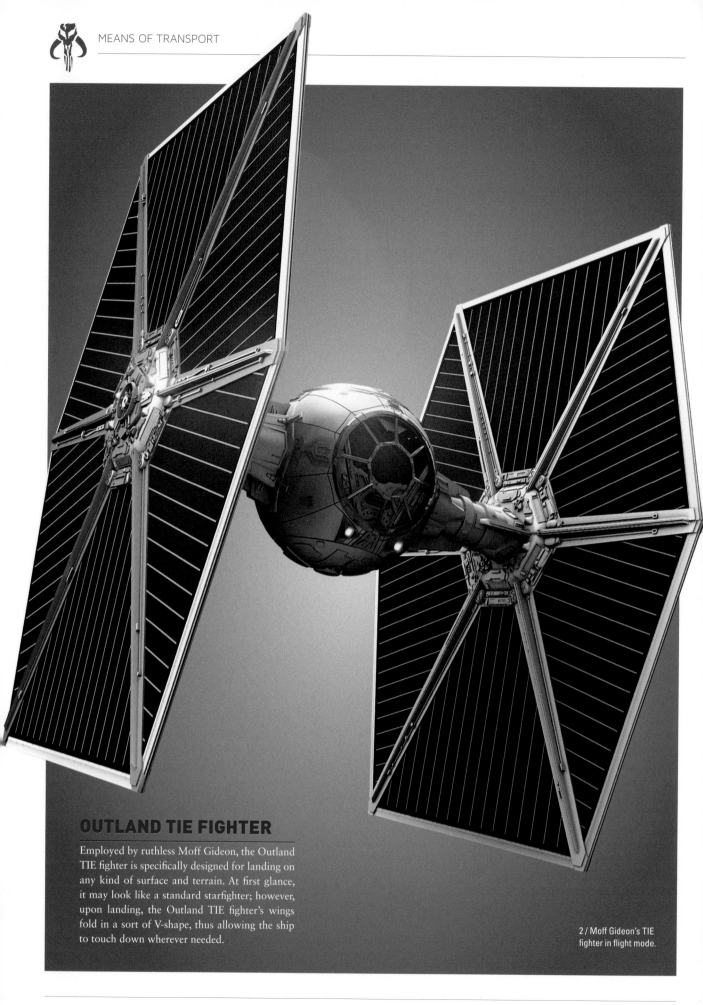

OUTLAND TIE FIGHTER

Employed by ruthless Moff Gideon, the Outland
TIE fighter is specifically designed for landing on
any kind of surface and terrain. At first glance,
it may look like a standard starfighter; however,
upon landing, the Outland TIE fighter's wings
fold in a sort of V-shape, thus allowing the ship
to touch down wherever needed.

2 / Moff Gideon's TIE
fighter in flight mode.

AT-ST RAIDER

A modified version of the more popular AT-ST walker, the two-legged armored craft was used by some raiders on planet Sorgan to invade the farmers' village. Equipped with two big laser cannons, the AT-ST was presumably the result of old Imperial wreckage getting refurbished for war purposes.

3 / The AT-ST raider covered in war paint.

JETPACK

6 /

Heavily employed by Mandalorians, jetpacks are aerial devices which allow their carrier to fly through the air—and quickly get out of trouble if needed. Carried on the back just like a regular backpack, some models also feature a top-loaded missile launcher that can prove very useful in particularly heated combat.

SPEEDER BIKE

Speeder bikes are the perfect vehicle for high-speed, open-air travels. Used by civilians and militaries alike —such as the Galactic Republic Army, Imperials, and Rebels—these craft rely on a repulsorlift technology which allows them to move above the ground. Often equipped with small blaster cannons, they can be used for scouting or survivor-hunting missions.

X-WING

Becoming the symbol of the Rebel Alliance during the Galactic Civil War, the X-wing starfighter takes its name from the distinctive X-shape formed by the wings when in attack position. Equipped with four laser cannons and two proton torpedo launchers, the spacecraft comes with a droid co-pilot—which probably wouldn't be Mando's favorite feature.

4 / Jetpacks give Mandalorians a tactical advantage in combat.

5 / Scout troopers lean against their speeder bikes.

6 / Iconic X-wing starfighters hurtle across the sky.

BLURRG

With their hostile expression, the two-legged creatures known as blurrgs may look quite intimidating. However, when tamed, they can be excellent beasts of burden thanks to their sturdy and robust body. Located on several planets across the galaxy, including Arvala-7, blurrgs can also be used as mounts—but first, one has to learn how to ride them…

LANDSPEEDER

Just like speeder bikes, landspeeders are on-world, ground vehicles which can hover about a meter above the ground. Often used to transport weapons as well as individuals, some speeders' engines are further powered by air-cooled thrust turbines.

7 /

7 / Female blurrgs eat their mates after copulation.

8 / Landspeeders are particularly useful on ice planets.

8 /

STAR WARS LIBRARY

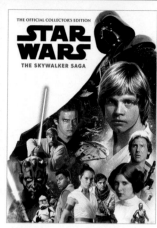

STAR WARS: THE EMPIRE STRIKES BACK: THE OFFICIAL COLLECTOR'S EDITION

THE MANDALORIAN THE ART AND IMAGERY VOLUME 2

STAR WARS: THE AGE OF RESISTANCE: THE OFFICIAL COLLECTOR'S EDITION

STAR WARS: THE SKYWALKER SAGA THE OFFICIAL MOVIE COMPANION

MARVEL LIBRARY

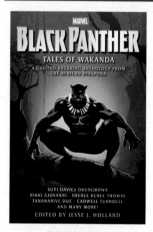

BLACK PANTHER TALES OF WAKANDA

MARVEL STUDIOS' THE COMPLETE AVENGERS

MARVEL STUDIOS' BLACK WIDOW

MARVEL: THE FIRST 80 YEARS